FROM SEA to SHINING SEA

TEXAS

ALEXANDRA HANSON-HARDING

Consultants

MELISSA N. MATUSEVICH, PH.D.
Curriculum and Instruction Specialist
Blacksburg, Virginia

JEANETTE LARSON
Austin Public Library
Austin, Texas

CHILDREN'S PRESS
A DIVISION OF SCHOLASTIC INC.

New York • Toronto • London • Auckland • Sydney • Mexico City
New Delhi • Hong Kong • Danbury, Connecticut

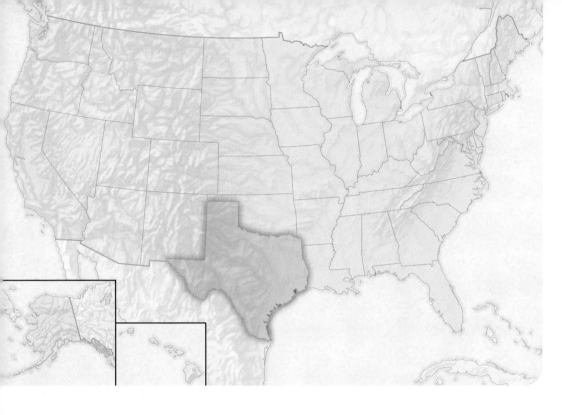

Texas is one of the four states
in the United States called
the Southwest. The other states
in this region are Arizona,
New Mexico, and Oklahoma.

Project Editor: Lewis K. Parker
Art Director: Marie O'Neill
Photo Researcher: Marybeth Kavanagh
Design: Robin West, Ox and Company, Inc.
Page 6 map and recipe art: Susan Hunt Yule
All other maps: XNR Productions, Inc.

Library of Congress Cataloging-in-Publication Data

Hanson-Harding, Alexandra.
        Texas/ Alexandra Hanson-Harding.
              p. cm—(From sea to shining sea)
        Includes bibliographical references (p.) and index.
        ISBN 0-516-22322-4
                1. Texas—Juvenile literature. [1. Texas.] I. Title.
                II. From sea to shining sea (Series)

F386.3. H38 2001
976.4—dc21   00-069386

TABLE of CONTENTS

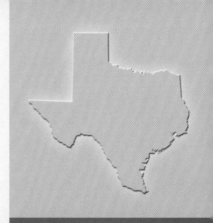

CHAPTER

ONE   Introducing the Lone Star State 4

TWO   The Land of Texas 7

THREE   Texas Through History 18

FOUR   Governing Texas 43

FIVE   The People and Places of Texas 53

Texas Almanac 70

Timeline 72

Gallery of Famous Texans 74

Glossary 75

For More Information 76

Index 77

INTRODUCING THE LONE STAR STATE

Many flags have been flown over the state of Texas.

Texas is a gigantic state. Only Alaska is larger. Texas is so big you could fit the states of Illinois, Indiana, Ohio, Pennsylvania, New York, New Jersey, and West Virginia inside its borders. You'd even have space left over for part of Rhode Island. If you take a car trip from Texarkana in the east to El Paso in the west, you'd better take lots of snacks for the road. It takes more than fifteen hours of driving to cross this state!

Texas hasn't always been a state of the United States. Texas has belonged to three other countries. At one time, Spain flew its flag over the land now called Texas. Then, France owned the territory. Later, Texas was part of Mexico.

Texas was once a country before it became a state. It was called the Republic of Texas. It coined its own money and had its own flag with one star on it. That's why Texas is nicknamed the Lone Star State. Texas was an independent country for almost ten years.

What do you think of when you think of Texas?

- Fierce and proud early Native Americans hunting buffalo
- Davy Crockett and William Travis defending the Alamo
- Cowboys working on huge cattle ranches
- The Rio Grande and the Red River winding through dry land
- Texas-born U.S. President Lyndon B. Johnson serving his country
- Vietnamese-Americans fishing for shrimp off the Gulf Coast
- The Dallas Cowboys winning the Super Bowl
- Armadillos waddling and roadrunners tracing K-shaped tracks
- Wells pumping oil and natural gas
- Huge farms where rice, cotton, and grapefruit grow
- Platters of beef barbecue, chicken fried steak, or Tex-Mex treats
- Astronauts being trained at the Johnson Space Center

Texas means many things. In this book, you'll read about some of the people and events that have helped to develop the Lone Star State. You'll discover the story of Texas.

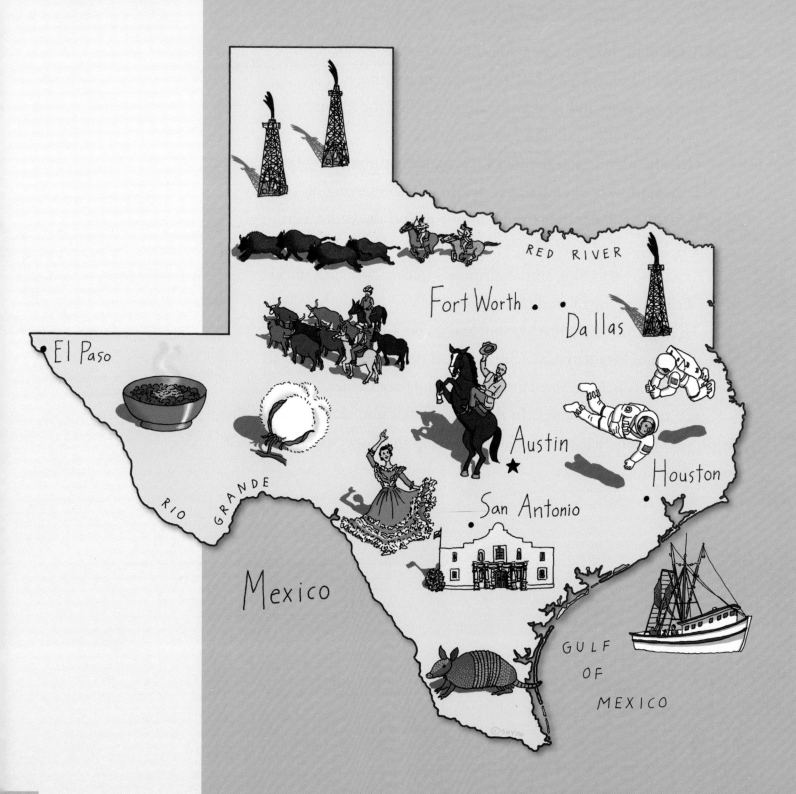

El Paso

RED RIVER

Fort Worth •

• Dallas

Austin

San Antonio

RIO GRANDE

Mexico

Houston

GULF OF MEXICO

CHAPTER TWO

THE LAND OF TEXAS

If there's one thing to remember about Texas, it's this—Texas is big. How big is it? At 267,277 total square miles (692,244 square kilometers), it's the second largest state in size after Alaska. It's bigger than all the countries of Europe (except for Russia). It's more than two hundred times larger than Rhode Island, the smallest state of the United States. However, there is much more to Texas than its size.

Texas has a variety of land-forms. Prairies, mountains, deserts, canyons — and miles and miles of beaches along its coastline.

This century plant grows in Big Bend National Park. Desert flowers bloom in the park from March through October.

The Rio Grande is famous for its recreational activities. These rafters enjoy the river far below towering canyon walls that stretch sixteen stories high.

If you look at a map, you'll see that Texas looks a little bit like a crooked, spinning top. It's wider in the middle than it is on the bottom or the top. The handle of the "top" is called the Panhandle. The bottom point is near the city of Brownsville. Four states border Texas: New Mexico and Oklahoma to the west and north, Arkansas and Louisiana to the north and east. A long curve of Texas borders the Gulf of Mexico.

Most of the southern and western borders of Texas are made by another nation, Mexico. This border is 1,240 miles (1,996 km) long. The Rio Grande, "Big River" in Spanish, which curves east, forms the border until it flows into the Gulf of Mexico.

Located in the Trans-Pecos region, Big Bend National Park gets its name from a U-shaped bend of the Rio Grande that borders the park. The park's 800,000 acres offer deep canyons plus beautiful desert scenery.

This visitor knows that a Texas beach is a good place to build a sand castle.

The state has more than 1,000 kinds of soil. Texas has wide prairies and rolling hills. Across these wide open spaces, fields of flowers can be seen for miles and miles. It has grand mountain peaks and deep canyons. Tumbleweeds roll through its deserts while its gorgeous beaches attract visitors from around the world.

Texas has basically four main physical regions. These areas are the Coastal Plains, the Central Plains, the Great Plains, and the Trans-Pecos Region. The first three regions are like a set of steps. They are big, broad plains broken up by a line of cliffs. The Trans-Pecos, however, is more rugged and mountainous.

THE COASTAL PLAINS

The eastern part of Texas is called the Coastal Plains. It makes up almost one-third of the state and covers about 300 miles (483 km) going west from the Gulf of Mexico.

The Coastal Plains region is divided into several smaller parts. The Piney Woods region is in northeast Texas, along the border between Texas and Louisiana. Because this area is covered by oak, pine, and sweet gum forests, it is home to lumber companies and paper mills. In the Piney Woods area, you'll find all of Texas's four national forests.

Where the Rio Grande flows into the Gulf of Mexico is a fertile valley. Farmers use water from the Rio Grande to irrigate their fields. They can farm all year around. A lot of the fruits and vegetables that you buy in supermarkets during the winter are grown here.

The edge of the Coastal Plains is a prairie. You won't find many trees on this flat, grassy land. Large herds of cattle graze here. Farmers grow crops in the rich soil of the prairie, such as wheat and cotton.

THE CENTRAL PLAINS

The Balcones Escarpment marks the southern boundary between the Coastal and Central Plains. This escarpment appears like a high balcony over the lowlands below. Several Texas cities are close to the dividing line between the Coastal Plains and the Central Plains. They include Dallas, Waco, and Austin. Austin is located in a pretty, hilly area simply called the Hill Country.

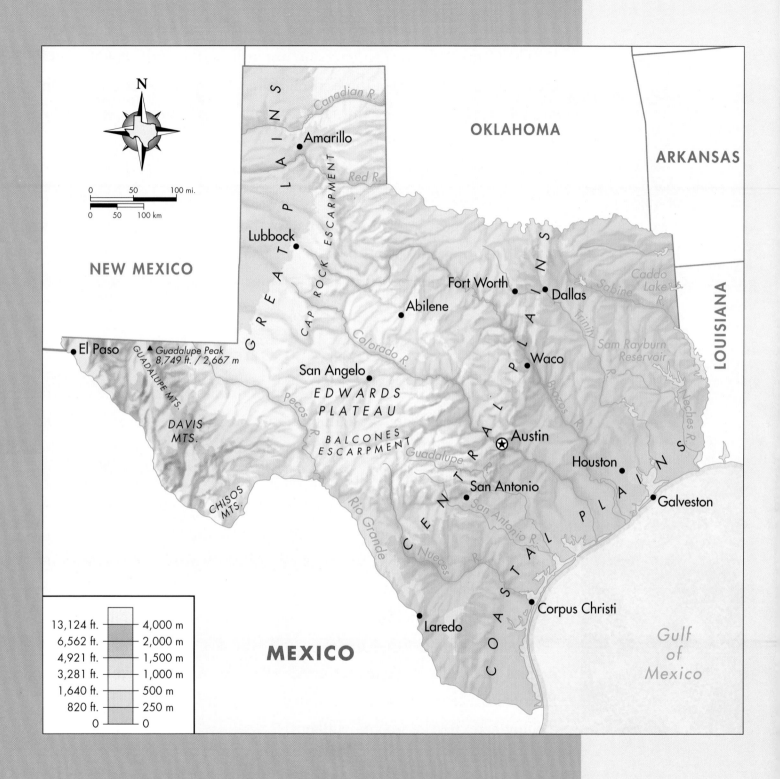

OKLAHOMA

ARKANSAS

NEW MEXICO

LOUISIANA

N

0   50   100 mi.
0   50   100 km

GREAT PLAINS

Canadian R.

Amarillo

Red R.

CAP ROCK ESCARPMENT

Lubbock

CENTRAL PLAINS

Fort Worth
Dallas

Sabine R.

Caddo Lake R.

Abilene

Colorado R.

Trinity R.

Sam Rayburn Reservoir

Waco

El Paso

Guadalupe Peak
8,749 ft. / 2,667 m

GUADALUPE MTS.

San Angelo

Pecos R.

EDWARDS PLATEAU

Brazos R.

Neches R.

DAVIS MTS.

BALCONES ESCARPMENT

Austin

Guadalupe R.

Houston

Galveston

CHISOS MTS.

Rio Grande

San Antonio

San Antonio R.

Nueces R.

COASTAL PLAINS

MEXICO

Laredo

Corpus Christi

Gulf
of
Mexico

13,124 ft.   4,000 m
6,562 ft.   2,000 m
4,921 ft.   1,500 m
3,281 ft.   1,000 m
1,640 ft.   500 m
820 ft.   250 m
0   0

The Central Plains are higher and not quite as flat as the land around the coast. In some parts of the Central Plains, forests have been cut down to make way for ranches and farms. Other parts have thin and rocky soil. Still others are wide prairies.

Many people make their living raising cattle, sheep, and goats here. One Texas city, San Angelo is called the "Wool and Mohair Capital." Texas Angora goats provide about half of the world's mohair. Farm crops include cotton, wheat, and peanuts. In fact, Texas is the second largest peanut producer in the United States.

GREAT PLAINS

Going even farther west, the land becomes drier and hillier. The eastern edge of the Great Plains has another escarpment, called the Cap Rock Escarpment. It is 200 miles (322 km) long, with cliffs that reach nearly 1,000 feet (305 meters) high.

This area is dry, but farmers have located water underground. The soil is rich and, with irrigation, farmers produce the most wheat, cotton, and sorghum in Texas. In fact, Texas is the main producer of cotton in the United States.

Part of the Great Plains is above an area called the Permian Basin. The Permian Basin is an underground lake that holds Texas's richest natural gas and petroleum resources. There is even a Permian Basin Petroleum Museum so visitors can learn more about the history of drilling here. It is located in Midland.

THE TRANS-PECOS REGION

The southwestern part of Texas is called the Trans-Pecos Region. The term means "across the Pecos River." The area is noted for its high mountains.

This chunk of Texas is as large as the state of South Carolina. However, few people live here. The climate is very hot and dry. High mountains also keep people from traveling easily from place to place. If you lived in Presidio, you'd have to drive ninety miles (144 km) for a pizza. The Chisos, Davis, and Guadalupe mountain ranges are here. So are Texas's highest mountain peaks. Seven of them are higher that 8,000 feet (2,438).

Oil wells that look like huge, metal grasshoppers pump petroleum out of the Permian Basin.

This view looks out over the rugged Chisos Mountains. The entire mountain range lies within Big Bend National Park.

TEXAS RIVERS AND OTHER WATERS

Almost everyone has heard of the Rio Grande. It is Texas's largest river and one of the longest rivers in North America. It forms the boundary between the United States and Mexico.

The Rio Grande (which is called Rio Brava del Norte in Mexico) starts in the mountains of Colorado and flows southeast. It takes a turn north in Texas's "Big Bend" region before heading southeast to pour into the Gulf of Mexico. The Rio Grande is 1,900 miles (3,057 km) long.

The Red River is more than 1,200 miles (1,931 km) long. It starts in New Mexico. As it flows eastward across the Panhandle, it forms the border between Texas and Oklahoma. Then this river empties into the Mississippi River.

The Brazos River flows almost all the way across Texas before it empties into the Gulf of Mexico. Texas's Colorado River provides water in the High Plains area. The Canadian River comes out of New Mexico, crosses the Panhandle, and flows into the Arkansas River.

Texas is even home to the shortest river in the United States. The Comal River starts in New Braunfels. It empties into the Guadalupe River after only two and a half miles (4 km).

Texas has many lakes and reservoirs where people can enjoy various water sports. For example, Sam Rayburn Reservoir is an 114,500 acre lake in the Angelina National Forest in East Texas. It is the largest body of water entirely within Texas. The Toledo Bend Reservoir between Texas and Louisiana covers 181,600 acres and has 1,264 miles (2,034 km) of coastline.

FIND OUT MORE

Caddo Lake spreads over 26,800 acres of Texas and Louisiana. The Caddo people believed this lake was formed by "shaking earth spirits" who were angry at a Caddo chief. What natural event might explain this story? What stories could you invent about how a body of water near you might have been formed?

CLIMATE

Texas is located in the southwest. It is one of the most southern of the states. That location means that Texas gets very hot in the summer and remains warm even in winter. Texas gets 248 days of sunshine each year. During the summer, the temperatures often top 100°F (37.8°C). The hottest temperature ever recorded in Texas was a scorching 120°F

(49°C). The state's weather can be very pleasant, especially in the spring, winter, and fall.

There is a saying: "Only fools and strangers predict weather in Texas." Weather can vary widely in this gigantic state. In some areas, the winter can become cold. For example, while farmers in the south are tending their grapefruit, people in Amarillo may be cleaning snow off their driveways. Brrrrr…The coldest temperature in Texas was -23°F (-30.5°C) in 1933.

Rainfall across Texas varies too. People in eastern Texas receive about 30 inches (76 cm) more rain than do residents of western Texas. On the average, Texas gets about 27 inches (67 cm) of rain a year. Some areas are prone to droughts. These droughts can kill crops and leave areas such as the Panhandle open to huge dust storms.

Texas gets its share of extreme weather. Northern Texas is part of "Tornado Alley"—a region in the center of the United States where most tornadoes form. Scientists who study tornadoes often come to Texas because the state has more tornadoes per year than does any other state.

Texas also faces danger from hurricanes. These storms come out of the Gulf of Mexico or cut across from Florida. Hurricanes can sometimes cause a great deal of damage in Texas. For example, in 1900, a hurricane with 120 mile-per-hour winds smashed into Galveston. A huge tidal wave swept over the city. It completely destroyed a third of the city, sweeping it out to sea. Worse yet, it killed about 6,000 people. At the time, this was the most deadly natural disaster in U.S. history. The people of Galveston built a seawall to protect against huge waves churned up by powerful storms.

In 2000, northern Texas experienced its worst drought ever. It suffered through more than ten weeks of sizzling heat with no rain. This drought broke the record for days without rain that was set in 1934! The temperatures remained over 100 degrees in parts of Texas for weeks on end.

FIND OUT MORE

In August 22-25, 1998, Hurricane Charley dumped eighteen inches (46 cm) of rain in Del Rio, Texas. Two-thirds of the city was flooded, and more than fifteen people were killed. What are some differences between hurricanes and tornadoes?

A flock of pelicans enjoy breezes coming off the water near Galveston.

CHAPTER THREE

TEXAS THROUGH HISTORY

Early people who lived in what is now Texas drew pictures on the walls of caves. These pictographs often showed the animals that they hunted or worshipped.

People have lived in Texas for at least 12,000 years. They arrived about the time that the last Ice Age occurred. Texas did not get the ice that covered much of North America at the time. However, the climate was cold and wet. Scientists believe that these early people were hunters who followed herds of mammoths and giant bison. They captured their prey by chasing the huge beasts over cliffs or by attacking them with spears while the animals drank at water holes.

About 7,000 years ago, early people began to settle in villages. In areas with good soil, they started to farm. They grew corn, beans, and squash. People who lived in areas without good soil or water continued to eat foods that they gathered.

People who lived in East Texas were the most successful farmers. These early people were the Caddos. They lived in the Neches River valley in the Piney Woods region. There they grew corn, sunflowers, and pumpkins. They also hunted deer and other game and fished for food. The Caddos built houses that looked like beehives. They covered the wooden frame of their houses with layers of grass.

The Caddos were organized into particular groups. There were priests, chiefs, and workers. They also built huge mounds near the center of their villages. The mounds seem to have been used as sacred temples and for burial. Over time, several Caddo tribes formed into a larger group called the Hasinai Confederacy. The Caddos called each other *tejas,* which meant friends. This word later gave Texas its name.

Another group of people lived in the desert of West Texas. They were known as the Pueblo Indians. They dug ditches to irrigate their gardens. Pueblos built adobe apartment houses. The adobe walls protected their homes against the changing temperature of the desert.

The Karankawa and Attacapa were Native American groups who lived along the Gulf Coast. They mainly fished for their food. The Coahuiltecan people settled in the southern part of Texas and the lower Rio Grande valley. They also built adobe homes.

Other groups also made their home in Texas. The Lipan Apache lived in South Central Texas. Mescalero Apache moved from areas that are now Arizona and New Mexico into Texas. Comanche traveled from the northern plains into the northern and central areas of Texas. They rode on horses to hunt buffalo.

FIND OUT MORE

A few years ago, scientists uncovered the skeleton of a Texas woman who had lived in the area 9,000 years ago. The skeleton had been carefully buried. It was found near Midland. The scientists named her Midland Minnie. How might life have been different for Midland Minnie than it is for you?

EXTRA! EXTRA!

Before the Pueblos started building adobe houses, they lived in pit houses. To make a pit house, they dug a round hole in the ground. Then they built a dome of wood, sticks, and mud over the hole. Their underground homes protected Pueblos from the heat of the day and the cold of the night.

TEXAS FIRSTS

- Estevanico may have been the first African to explore what is now the United States.
- William Gebhardt invented the first commercial chili powder here in 1894.
- Jack Kilby of Texas Instruments invented the silicon computer chip in 1958. In 1965, he and other inventors created the first hand-held electronic calculator.
- Dr. Pepper was invented in Waco in 1885 by a pharmacist. The Frito corn chip was also invented in Texas. Other Texan foods include fajitas and nachos.

Cabeza de Vaca and his men made a trek through Texas, New Mexico, and Arizona. His adventure tales became the legend of the Seven Golden Cities of Cibola.

EUROPEAN EXPLORERS ARRIVE

The first Europeans to arrive in Texas were Spanish explorers. In the 1500s, Spanish soldiers had conquered Mexico. Álonso Alvarez de Piñeda became the first European to make maps of the coastline of Texas in 1519.

In 1528, a group of Spanish explorers were shipwrecked off the coast of Texas. The group included a Spaniard named Alvar Núñez Cabeza de Vaca and an African named Estevanico.

These explorers lived among Texas's Indians for seven years. Then Estevanico and Cabeza de Vaca traveled all over Texas as traders and healers. They met with many different groups of Native Americans, until they finally made it to Mexico. Later, Cabeza de Vaca wrote letters to the king of Spain telling about his adventures. In 1543, the letters were collected in a book, which encouraged Spanish interest in exploring and settling the Texas area.

Believing that the New World was rich in gold, other Spanish explorers sailed to North America. Francisco Vásquez de Coronado led a group of Spanish soldiers through the Texas Panhandle in 1540. From 1541 to 1543, so did explorer Hernando de Soto. Neither of them found gold.

The Spanish weren't the only Europeans interested in North America. In 1684, René-Robert Cavelier, Sieur de La Salle led a group of 300 French colonists to North America. They were supposed to settle near the mouth of the Mississippi River. Instead, they were shipwrecked near Matagorda Bay, on the coast of Texas. There, they built a fort called Fort Saint Louis. For a while, the French flag flew over Texas. However, before long, diseases, starvation, and attacks from Native Americans had destroyed the fort.

For several years, de Vaca and his companions lived with Native Americans.

This engraving shows La Salle after being shipwrecked along the Texas coast. La Salle established Fort St. Louis, which provided France's claim to what is now Texas.

THE SPANISH SETTLE TEXAS

In 1682, the Spanish began to set up missions in Texas. A Catholic priest called a *padre* ("father" in Spanish) led each mission. A mission provided shelter, clothing, and food for Native Americans who came into the fort to learn about the Catholic faith. Besides teaching Native Americans about their religion, the priests taught them how to grow other crops, such as peas, onions, and watermelon. The priests also taught the Native Americans skills, such as weaving cloth and building with stone.

However, few Native Americans liked mission life for long. Many felt that they were treated as servants and their freedom was restricted. The Spanish built forts just outside the missions to defend themselves against attacks by hostile Native Americans. Many groups, such as Comanches, stayed in missions as protection against their enemies—other tribes such as Apaches.

In the 1700s, herding cattle became an important kind of work. Longhorn cattle brought by early settlers had escaped into the wild. The cattle grew fat on the endless fields of prairie grass. Although the cattle population grew quickly, the human population settlement of Texas expanded very slowly. By 1793, only about 7,000 settlers lived there.

(opposite)
Mission de la Ysleta was the first Spanish mission in Texas. It was built in 1682 near what is now El Paso.

In the early days of Texas, longhorn cattle roamed in great herds across the plains.

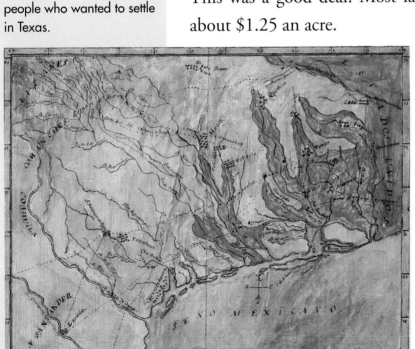

Stephen F. Austin is called the "Father of Texas."

Austin used this map to divide land into sections for people who wanted to settle in Texas.

MEXICO BECOMES INDEPENDENT

In 1821, Mexico became independent from Spain. Now, Texas was part of the Republic of Mexico. The Mexican government was eager to have more people live in Texas. More people in Texas also meant more goods would be traded and more taxes could be paid to the Mexican government. The government offered large sections of land to people who wanted to settle in Texas.

In 1821, Stephen F. Austin got permission from Mexico to bring settlers to Texas—if the settlers would become Mexican citizens and Roman Catholics. To find settlers, Stephen F. Austin put ads in newspapers. He offered to sell land in Texas at about twelve cents an acre. This was a good deal. Most land in the United States was selling for about $1.25 an acre.

By 1825, about 300 families had moved to Texas and formed a colony. The colony was called San Felipe de Austin. Because these colonists were the first large, English-speaking group to settle in Texas, they are called the Old Three Hundred. San Felipe de Austin was the official start of the American settlement of Texas.

Soon, more and more people began to move there from other states. When they left their homes, many

People traveled from the East in covered wagons to settle in Texas.

people put signs that said "G.T.T." —Gone to Texas—in their windows. Immigrant families also began to arrive from European countries. Some Mexicans also moved north to Texas.

FIND OUT MORE

Gail Borden was a member of Austin's colony. He noticed that many babies died when they drank spoiled milk. At that time, there was no way to keep milk fresh. Bordon invented a machine that made condensed milk. The machine took the water out of milk so it could be safely stored. The invention made him rich. How is milk kept fresh today?

As soon as large numbers of Americans began settling in Texas, tensions increased between the Mexican government and the settlers. The government was upset that the settlers were trading mainly with the United States and not with Mexico. Many Mexican officials feared that the United States wanted to take over Texas.

On the other hand, the settlers were angry that the Mexican schools were only taught in Spanish and not English. They were also unhappy that the Mexican government had outlawed slavery.

Most of the American settlers had come from Southern states. In those states, slavery was legal. African-American slaves were treated as property that could be bought and sold. Slaves did hard work that their owners didn't want to do. The Americans wanted to use slaves to work on large cotton farms and ranches in Texas. The settlers wanted to make their own rules and laws. In 1830, the Mexican government said that no more Americans could settle in Texas.

In 1833, Stephen F. Austin presented a list of grievances (complaints) to Mexico's government. Instead of listening, members of the government threw Austin into jail. Also that year, General Antonio López de Santa Anna became Mexico's president. He quickly became its dictator. In 1835, Austin was released. When Austin returned to Texas, he said, "War is our only recourse. There is no other, for we must defend our rights, ourselves, and our country."

By 1836, about 50,000 people were living in Texas. They outnumbered Mexican settlers at least six to one. The American settlers, who called themselves "Texians," prepared to fight for their independence.

"COME AND TAKE IT"

General Santa Anna sent soldiers to stop the Texians. On October 2, 1835, 100 soldiers tried to seize a cannon in the town of Gonzales. The Texians put up a flag that read "Come and Take It." They loaded the cannon with scrap metal. Then they shot it at the soldiers. The Mexicans retreated without taking the cannon. It was the shot that started the Texas revolution.

A few months later, on February 23, 1836, 4,000 Mexican soldiers trapped about 180 Texian rebels inside the Alamo. The Alamo was the chapel of a former mission in San Antonio. Colonel William B. Travis, who commanded the fort, wrote a letter asking for help. "I shall never surrender or retreat . . . Victory or death," he wrote.

Against Santa Anna's huge army, Travis's troops held on for thirteen days. They ran out of food, water, and ammunition. In the end, Mexican troops stormed the Alamo. They slaughtered every last one of the Alamo's defenders, including Colonel Travis and Davy Crockett.

Meanwhile, on March 1, 1836, a group of Texian leaders had gathered to quickly write the Texas Declaration of Independence. It was written overnight, then adopted by the delegates of the convention the following day. It said, in no uncertain terms, "We, therefore . . . declare,

Davy Crockett was one of the men who died at the Alamo. He had been an outdoorsman and a Congressman from Tennessee before going to defend the Alamo.

This drawing shows the defeat of the rebels at the Alamo. For thirteen days, the 189 rebels held out against more than 3,000 Mexican soldiers.

that our political connection with the Mexican nation has forever ended, and that the people of Texas do now constitute a free, Sovereign, and independent republic."

This death of the Alamo defenders outraged the Texians. General Sam Houston gathered together Americans who wanted to fight. Then he retreated south. His men were confused and upset. Many soldiers wondered why the general was fleeing instead of fighting.

On April 21, 1836, Houston announced that it was time to fight. "Remember the Alamo!" he told them. "Victory or Death!"

Sam Houston's defeat of the Mexican army at San Jacinto is celebrated in this painting.

Houston had only 783 men while Santa Anna had 1,400. However, Houston trapped the Mexican troops on land that was surrounded by water on three sides. He also attacked while the Mexicans were taking their afternoon nap. After a fierce 19-minute attack, the Mexicans fled. General Santa Anna ran away too, disguised as a common soldier. He was soon captured. With victory at the Battle of San Jacinto, the Texians had won the war. The Republic of Texas was born.

TEXAS REPUBLIC

The Republic of Texas faced many challenges. Its leaders had to set up a government, create money, and choose a capital. Even more important, it had to defend its borders from attacks from Mexico. Texans invaded Mexico in return. Tensions between the two neighbors were high.

To defend Texas and to keep order, Stephen F. Austin set up a special police force called the Texas Rangers. The rangers were organized to protect ranchers from Indian attacks. They also served as a kind of police force, and guarded Texas's border against Mexico. The Rangers earned $1.25 a day and had to provide their own horses, food, and guns. They roved over the land dealing out rough "frontier justice." One ranger reported to his commanding officer, "Had a fight with raiders, killed twelve and captured two hundred and sixty five beeves [cows]. Wish you were here." They stopped bandits and helped to bring law and order to a wild untamed land.

The Texas Rangers were first organized in 1835. Today, Texas Rangers still work to track down dangerous criminals and to help protect the governor.

Many Native Americans began to move to Texas, too, especially Apaches and Comanches. They had been pushed further west as more and more settlers also moved west. These Native Americans were experts at riding horses and were brave fighters. They didn't like settlers taking over land that they needed for hunting buffalo.

Texas's first president, Sam Houston, liked the Indians. The second president, Mirabeau Lamar, declared he wanted Native Americans out of Texas. His choice of a new capital, Austin, was north of where most of Texas's residents lived. In fact, it overlooked land that the Comanches claimed as their own.

The settlers and the Native Americans didn't get along very well. In 1840, some Comanche leaders and their wives were killed in San Antonio, after talks about trading captives failed. In revenge, Comanche fighters attacked settlers, stole horses, and burned settlements in Texas's Guadalupe Valley. After Texas volunteers formed a small army, they chased the Comanches. On August 11, 1840, they reached the Comanches at a place called Plum Creek. They fought, and the settlers won. The Comanches were forced to retreat west. Battles between settlers and Native Americans would continue for decades.

The challenges were overwhelming for the people of Texas. The new republic was squeezed between a hostile Mexico and hostile Native Americans, with wide spaces and few people.

The legislature of the Texas Republic had to find a solution. Some legislators wanted Texas to stay a republic. They said it would be good if Texas could keep its own government. They also said that Texas could make treaties with other nations that might make it rich. Others, including Sam Houston, thought Texas should be a state. That way, Texas could trade with other states. The United States could also help defend Texas. Part of the taxes that people all over the United States paid could be used to help develop Texas. Finally, Texas's legislature decided to become part of the United States.

However, even when Texas decided to try to become a state, many people in the United States were worried about the idea. One reason was that many Americans were afraid of risking war with Mexico. Some members of Congress did not want Texas to join the United States because Texas would be a slave-owning state. Finally, Sam Houston suggested another plan. He argued that Texas might join with a European country instead of with the United States. That was enough for U.S. President James Polk. He signed a law making Texas the 28th state on December 29, 1845.

Texas's population grew quickly once it became a state. In 1850, 212,000 people lived in Texas. Ten years later, the number had nearly tripled, to 600,000 people. Over time, more and more immigrants began arriving in Texas.

The U.S. Census taken in 1860 showed that 43,422 European-born people lived in Texas. For example, German immigrants farmed in settlements of New Braunfels, Fredericksburg, and Sisterdale. French immigrants founded Castroville in Medina County. They also built the towns of Vandenberg and D'Hanis. The French colony of La Reunion became the site of Dallas. Polish immigrants settled the town of Panna Maria and Irish immigrants settled in Refugio. Norwegians settled in Brownsboro and Clifton, which has been called "The Norwegian Capital of Texas." Each immigrant group enriched Texas culture with their special traditions, languages, and music.

More Mexicans moved into Texas, too. By 1860, more than 12,000 Mexicans were landowners in Texas. Many became farmers in the Rio Grande Valley. Other Mexican Americans lived in the towns of San Antonio, El Paso, and Laredo.

On April 25, 1846, the Mexican–American war started over the boundaries between Texas and Mexico. In 1848, Mexico signed a peace treaty to set Texas's southern boundary at the Rio Grande River. The United States also received the whole northern half of Mexico—land that now has become the states of Arizona, California, Nevada, New Mexico, and Utah. But even then, Texas boundaries were much larger than they were today. A few years later, as part of the Compromise of 1850, Texas gave a third of its remaining land to the U.S. Government for $10 million from the United States. Texas needed the money to pay off its public debts. The land later became parts of five states—New Mexico, Oklahoma, Kansas, Colorado, and Wyoming.

THE CIVIL WAR

Texas wasn't a state very long before war broke out again. For a long time, the Northern and Southern states of the United States had disagreed about slavery. Northern states wanted to end slavery, but the Southern states supported slavery. Farming was not as important in the Northern states as it was in the South. In the Northern states many people were now working in factories. In the South, many people argued that their farms would go broke without the free labor of slaves.

In 1861, many Southern states seceded (broke away) from the United States and formed their own nation, the Confederate States of America. Texas governor, Sam Houston, was against leaving the United States. "To secede [break away] from the Union and set up another government would cause war," he said. "If [the U.S.] does not whip you by guns, powder, and steel, she will starve you to death."

The Texas legislature voted for the state to become a member of the Confederacy on February 1, 1861. Houston was removed from office.

Few battles were fought in Texas during the Civil War, but more than 70,000 Texas men joined the Confederate Army. Texas also supplied food and other goods for the Confederate side.

In April, 1865, the Southern armies surrendered and the Civil War ended. It took time for the

Texas was a member of the Confederate States of America. Texas soldiers defeated Union forces at Galveston in 1863.

news to reach Texas. A month after the war officially ended, the Battle of Palmito Ranch was fought in Texas. It was the last battle of the Civil War.

Texas's many slaves were also late to know the good news that slavery was over. On June 19, 1865, almost a month after the Civil War was over, General Gordon Granger of the Union army arrived in Galveston. He announced, "The people of Texas are informed that … all slaves are free." Upon hearing the news, African-Americans began to celebrate. "Juneteenth" (for June nineteenth) is now a state holiday in Texas.

Many cowboys were African-American. Here, a cowboy pulls a cow that has become stuck in mud.

HOME ON THE RANGE

In 1866, many former Confederate soldiers returned to Texas to find few jobs awaiting them after the war. However, some clever business owners saw an opportunity in Texas's giant herds of longhorn cattle. They started "cattle drives" to move the longhorns to markets farther north. Many former soldiers became cowboys driving cattle to railroad stations in Texas. There, cattle was shipped to stockyards in the North. Texas cowboys became famous. Their rugged life was celebrated in

songs and stories. Not all of the cowboys were returning Civil War soldiers. Many were former slaves. And many were Mexican Americans.

When cattle drives started, cattle grazed on land that was not owned by anyone. It was a large, open range. Most of this cattle didn't have brands. They were considered mavericks. Anyone could take and brand cattle as his or her own. However, as cattle drives made some ranch owners wealthy and barbed wire was invented, all that changed. The invention of barbed wire led to a cheap way to divide up the open range.

A small group of rich men made deals to buy up huge pieces of land. Then, they could own the large herds that grazed in these big ranches. One of these ranches, The King Ranch, is larger than the state of

It was long and hot work driving cattle to markets. Here, cowboys have herded the cows to a river where they can drink.

EXTRA! EXTRA!

A person who is independent and doesn't follow the crowd is sometimes called a "maverick." The word comes from Sam Maverick. He was a rancher who refused to put a brand on his cattle. When cowboys found a longhorn cow that wasn't branded, they said, "Must be one of Maverick's." He claimed any unbranded cows as his own.

Rhode Island. It is still operating today. Santa Gertrudis cattle were also developed at the King Ranch. This breed, or type, was the first breed of cattle produced in the United States. They were developed from two other breeds called Brahmin and shorthorn cattle and were known for growing quickly, for their good tempers, and for their solid red color.

In the 1860s and '70s, Buffalo Soldiers patrolled Texas against attacks from Native Americans. These were U.S. soldiers who were African-American. They fought for the United States during the long struggles with Native Americans. Native American groups gave them the nickname "Buffalo Soldiers" because of their courage, which was like that of the buffalo. The Buffalo Soldiers' duty was not a pleasant one, but it helped prove to the rest of the United States that African-American soldiers could be just as skilled and brave as non-African-American soldiers. By 1875, most Native Americans had been forced from Texas to reservations in Oklahoma.

After the Civil War, the U.S. Congress made the former Confederate states develop new constitutions. Then, these states could be admitted back into the Union. In 1870, Texas was readmitted into the United States. And by 1881, the capitol building was being built in Austin. At that time, people didn't realize it, but a big change and a big opportunity would soon occur in Texas—the discovery of oil.

GUSHER!

The first major oil field in Texas was at Corsicana. In 1894 workers were trying to dig a new water well. Instead of finding water, they struck oil. Before long there were five oil wells that produced 1,500 barrels of oil a year. Within six years, wells in Corsicana were producing 850,000 barrels of oil a year. The pool of oil under Corsicana was about five miles long and two miles wide.

J.S. Cullinan, a businessman in Pennsylvania, heard about the oil strike in Texas. He came to Texas and built a refinery. A refinery contains machines that turn oil into kerosene and gasoline. Cullinan also developed a way for trains to use oil instead of coal as a fuel. He started a business called the Texas Fuel Company. It later became known as Texaco, Inc., one of the largest oil companies in the world.

Oil that was discovered at Spindletop is a better-known discovery. On January 10, 1901, oil gushed out of a well at the Spindletop oil field near Beaumont. This well produced 17 million barrels of oil in 1901. Within a year, more than one hundred other oil wells were in the same area. The discovery at Spindletop showed that finding oil in Texas was not an accident. A search for oil spread throughout Texas, with big companies looking to make huge profits. The Texas oil boom had started.

Soon, Beaumont became a boomtown. In two years, its population grew from 9,000 to 50,000. Before long, many parts of the state would prove to have large oil deposits. Oil has made much of the state rich. Its fortunes rose and shrank with the oil industry.

The Spindletop gusher started the oil boom in Texas. The fountain of oil shot 200 feet into the air.

Since then, Texas has had many ups and downs. During World War I (1914-1918), more than 200,000 Texans served in the armed services. Texas was hard hit by the Great Depression (1929-1934), a time of economic troubles in the United States and around the world. When the New York Stock Market crashed, banks closed throughout the country. Thousands of Texans lost their jobs as businesses failed.

Many Texas farmers had a hard time for a different reason. During the Depression, there was a terrible drought in parts of Texas. The dry land turned Texas into part of the "Dust Bowl"—an area where no crops grew and winds whipped loose dirt into sandstorms. Many farmers left Texas to try to find work in California and other places.

About 750,000 Texans served in World War II (1939-1945), including 12,000 women. In fact, Texas had the only all-women air base. It was located at Sweetwater. In the war, thirty-six Texans won the Congressional Medal of Honor, the highest U.S. military award. An actor in many cowboy movies, Audie Murphy, who grew up in Kingston, was the most decorated soldier of World War II for his bravery. Texan industries helped by making explosives and plastic products at chemical factories. Texans built ships and airplanes in factories. Texas farms grew even more wheat and corn to feed soldiers fighting in other countries. World War II brought the Great Depression to an end as many people found work in factories.

In the 1950s, Texas born Dwight D. Eisenhower became the 34th U.S. President. During Eisenhower's presidency, the Civil

Texas has provided the United States with four presidents. Dwight Eisenhower (1890–1969) was the first president to come from Texas. He was born in Denison.

Rights movement began to change life for Texas's African-Americans. Texas laws forced whites and African-Americans to be segregated. African-Americans could not use public schools, restaurants, restrooms, theaters, hotels, or drinking fountains that were meant for whites. In the 1950s and 1960s, African-Americans began to struggle for their civil rights as citizens of the United States. The University of Texas became desegregated in 1950. Some civil rights leaders also came from Texas. James Farmer is one of them. He founded an important organization called the Congress for Racial Equality (CORE) that fought for change.

When John F. Kennedy became U.S. President after Eisenhower, he chose Texas native Lyndon Baines Johnson to be vice president. On November 22, 1963, Kennedy was assassinated in Dallas. A few hours later, Johnson was sworn in as the 36th President.

In 1964, the Manned Space Center was opened in Houston, Texas. It was later renamed the Lyndon B. Johnson Space Center in honor of Johnson's efforts to promote space exploration. This center became the command post as astronauts blasted into space.

EXTRA! EXTRA!

Tranquility Park in downtown Houston is named for the place on the moon where astronauts first landed. Written in fifteen languages, bronze plaques at the park's entrances tell about the journey to the moon.

The Texas State Fair is the largest state fair in the nation. A 52-foot plastic cowboy named Big Tex welcomes visitors to the fair.

When astronauts landed on the moon on July 20, 1969, the first word they spoke was the name of a Texas city. Why? Because the astronauts were letting people in Houston know that they were okay. The whole sentence was, "Houston, Tranquility Base here. The Eagle has landed."

In 1989, George Bush, an oil company executive who had served as a congressman from Texas, became the 41st president. His son, George W. Bush, the governor of Texas, was elected president in 2000.

How is Texas doing today? Modern-day Texas has its share of problems. According to the U.S. Department of Energy, Houston and Southern California have the worst air pollution problems in the country.

Air pollution affects other parts of Texas as well. Even remote Big Bend National Park has so many smoggy days that experts are studying how to cut down on pollution there. Houston's ship channel is the fifth most polluted in the United States. Many of Texas's waterways, including the Rio Grande, have serious pollution problems as well. Nearly one out of every four Texans lacks health insurance—giving the state the highest rate of people without insurance in the United States.

Still Texas has a lot to be proud of. It is one of the fastest-growing states in the country, and it has a booming economy. Once, Texas's economy depended mostly on oil prices. Not any more. Texas has changed so that now it gets its money from many different industries. Texas's gross state product (GSP) is nearly $700 billion a year. If the state of Texas were an independent country, it would be one of the richest countries in the world. Texas also trades many of its goods and services—from wool to computers—with countries around the world. Its largest trading partners are Canada, Mexico, and Taiwan.

Texas boasts one of the largest state fairs in the country. The state also continues to lead in music, arts, sports, and business. It has creative, successful people. They include Texas actors such as

WHAT'S IN A NAME?

The names of many places in Texas have interesting origins.

Name	Come From or Means
Amarillo	"Yellow" in Spanish
Austin	Stephen F. Austin, the "Father of Texas"
Corpus Christi	"body of Christ" in Spanish
El Paso	"The Pass of the North" in Spanish (for pass cut by Rio Grande through Franklin Mountains)
Houston	Sam Houston, governor of Texas (1859-1861)
Rio Grande	Spanish for "big river"
Borden	Gail Borden, inventor of condensed milk
Nacogdoches	Nacogdoche Indians who once lived there
Texas	Tejas, a Caddo word meaning friend
Victoria	Guadalupe Victoria, first president of Mexico
Waxahachie	Native American word meaning "cow creek"

A famous dance group in New York City is the Alvin Ailey Dance Troupe. It was started by Alvin Ailey, a Texan.

Tommy Lee Jones and Jennifer Love Hewitt, comedians like Steve Martin, and singers like Willie Nelson. A Texas superstar athlete is Mia Hamm of the U.S. Women's Soccer Team. She helped the team capture the 1999 Women's World Cup. She was born in Alabama, but she calls Texas her home. Michael Dell is one of those creative business people. In 1984, Dell started selling computers from his room at the University of Texas in Austin. Now Dell Computers is one of the top personal computer makers in the world. It has more than 34,000 employees. It's that kind of independent, pioneering spirit that continues to push Texas forward today.

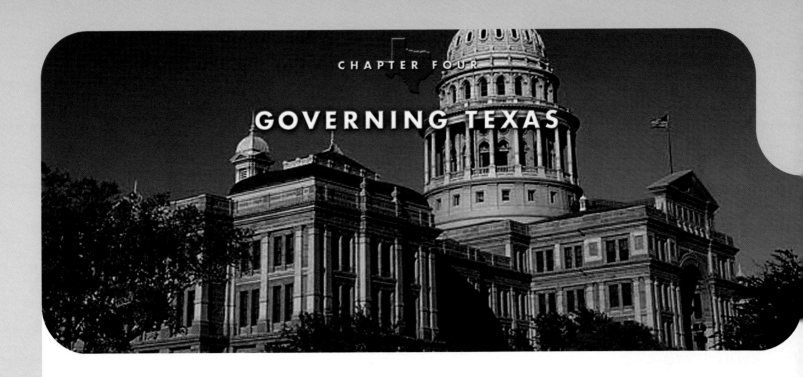

CHAPTER FOUR

GOVERNING TEXAS

Texans have always loved their freedom. Texas settlers may have been thinking about this spirit when Texan leaders like José Antonio Navarro helped to create their first constitution in 1836. This constitution marked Texas's independence. Texans have written several constitutions since then. The 1876 constitution is the one used today. Texans thought that the previous constitutions gave too much power to the state government. They wrote the 1876 constitution to give more power to the people.

The Texas constitution is a document which lays out the laws and principles that govern the state. The rights of the people of Texas are in a part of the Constitution called the Bill of Rights. The Constitution also defines how the government should operate. For example, it separates the powers of the government into the legislative, executive, and judicial branches.

The state capitol building in Austin is the largest in the United States.

43

Visitors to the legislative chambers can sit in the galleries above the floor.

THE LEGISLATIVE

The legislative branch makes laws, such as those to pay for schools or to build roads. It also makes up the budget to run all the services of the state.

The people elect members of this branch of government. The legislative branch is made of the House of Representatives and the Senate. The House has 150 members. Each member is elected to serve a two-year term. There are thirty-one senators. Each senator is elected for a four-year term. The legislature meets for about five months every other year.

THE EXECUTIVE

The executive branch is in charge of making sure the laws are carried out. The executive branch is made up of the governor, the secretary of state, the attorney general, the lieutenant governor, and two other officials. The governor is the leader of the executive branch. He or she is elected by the people. The governor can propose laws or veto (say no to) laws that the legislature passed. The lieutenant governor also serves as the president of the state Senate, and gets to vote on all bills.

The governor is elected every four years. There is no limit on how many times a governor can be elected. The governor's power is limited though. Many state officials, such as the lieutenant governor, are also elected. They may be members of a different political party than the governor. This may make it difficult for the governor to get the support of all the important state officials.

The eyes of the nation focused on Texas when Governor George W. Bush campaigned for the presidency. President Bush was sworn in as the 43rd U.S. President on January 20, 2001.

The judicial branch interprets state laws. The courts make up the judicial branch. They decide whether someone has broken the law and determine the punishment.

There are many levels to Texas's court system. The lowest level of courts are Municipal Courts and Justice of the Peace courts. The kinds of cases that come to these kinds of courts are cases that have to do with breaking city laws. One example is if people put out their garbage at the wrong time, or have a dangerous dog, the court might say they should be fined. Justice of the Peace courts might also handle small civil matters, like a problem between two neighbors.

The next level of courts are the county level courts. Their overall purpose is to oversee law matters on a county level. The county judge is the head of the county government. Some of these courts oversee matters such as making a grown-up a guardian for a child who has no parents.

Above the county level courts are the Texas District Courts. These are very important. Felony (major crime) cases are tried in these courts. So are divorce cases, civil cases where one party wants more than $200 from the other, and other kinds of cases.

If people are unhappy with the outcome of a trial in a district or a

FIND OUT MORE

Texas courts handle two kinds of cases—civil and criminal. Most civil cases are between two people or two groups of people. A civil case might involve one person suing another person over an auto accident. A divorce is another kind of civil case. A criminal case is one where a person is charged with breaking a law. There are two types of criminal cases. (1) A felony is a serious crime, such as robbery or murder. (2) A misdemeanor case is less serious, such as disturbing the peace or driving without a license. If someone was on trial for stealing a woman's pocketbook, would that be a criminal case or a civil case?

county court, they can go to a Court of Appeals. There are fourteen of these courts. Usually, a panel of three judges will hear what was decided in the lower court, and why the person disagrees with the decision. Then, they will make their own judgment.

If the person is still not satisfied, he or she can try to take the case to the top level in Texas's judicial system. The top level is divided into two parts, the Court of Criminal Appeals and the Supreme Court.

The Court of Criminal Appeals is made up of nine members. The most serious kind of cases they have to decide is whether someone should get the death penalty.

The Supreme Court oversees civil case appeals. The Supreme Court of Texas is made up of nine members. The Supreme Court also has the responsibility of making sure that Texas's judicial system is fair and efficient.

TAKE A TOUR OF AUSTIN, THE STATE CAPITAL

Texas has the largest capitol building of any state. It is even taller than the U.S. Capitol building in Washington, D.C.!

The capitol in Austin is made of pink Texas granite. It is more than 300 feet tall (91.5 m) and 566 feet long (172.5 m). On top of the building's round iron dome is a 16-foot-tall (4.88 m) aluminum statue called the Goddess of Liberty. The capitol was built between 1885 and 1888. Inside the capitol are life-size statues of Stephen F. Austin and Sam Houston. If you visit the capitol, you can watch legislators talk about new laws.

TEXAS STATE GOVERNMENT

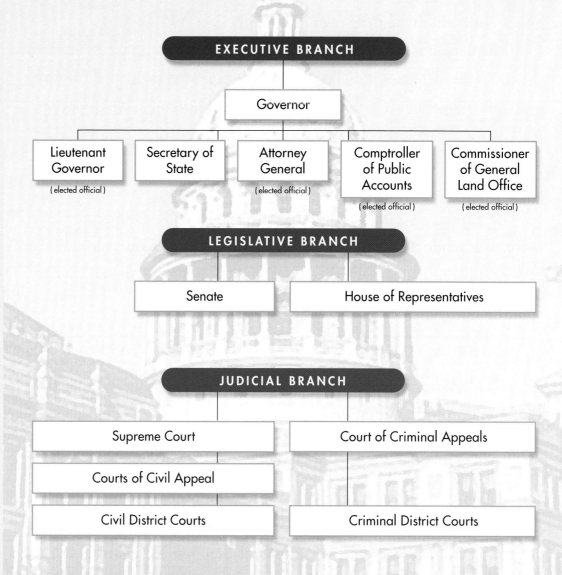

EXECUTIVE BRANCH

Governor

Lieutenant Governor	Secretary of State	Attorney General	Comptroller of Public Accounts	Commissioner of General Land Office
(elected official)		(elected official)	(elected official)	(elected official)

LEGISLATIVE BRANCH

Senate

House of Representatives

JUDICIAL BRANCH

Supreme Court

Court of Criminal Appeals

Courts of Civil Appeal

Civil District Courts

Criminal District Courts

TEXAS GOVERNORS

Name	Term	Name	Term
J. Pinckney Henderson	1846–1847	Oscar B. Colquitt	1911–1915
George T. Wood	1847–1849	James E. Ferguson	1915–1917
P. Hansborough Bell	1849–1853	William P. Hobby	1917–1921
Elisha M. Pease	1853–1857	Pat M. Neff	1921–1925
Hardin R. Runnels	1857–1859	Miriam A. Ferguson	1925–1927
Sam Houston	1859–1861	Dan Moody	1927–1931
Francis R. Lubbock	1861–1863	Ross Sterling	1931–1933
Pendleton Murrah	1863–1865	Miriam A. Ferguson	1933–1935
Under federal military rule	1865	James V. Allred	1935–1939
Andrew J. Hamilton	1865–1866*	W. Lee O'Daniel	1939–1941
James W. Throckmorton	1866–1867*	Coke R. Stevenson	1941–1947
Elisha M. Pease	1867–1869	Beauford H. Jester	1947–1949
Under federal military rule	1869–1870	Allan Shivers	1949–1957
Edmund J. Davis	1870–1874	Price Daniel	1957–1963
Richard Coke	1874–1876	John B. Connolly	1963–1969
Richard B. Hubbard	1876–1879	Preston Smith	1969–1973
Oran M. Roberts	1879–1883	Dolph Briscoe	1973–1979
John Ireland	1883–1887	Bill Clements	1979–1983
Lawrence S. Ross	1887–1891	Mark White	1983–1987
James S. Hogg	1891–1895	Bill Clements	1987–1991
Charles A. Culberson	1895–1899	Ann W. Richards	1991–1995
Joseph D. Sayers	1899–1903	George W. Bush	1995–2000
S.W.T. Lanham	1903–1907	Rick Perry	2000–
Thomas M. Campbell	1907–1911	*Confederate state governors	

Traditional Mexican dancing often takes place during festivals in Austin.

It took 15,000 railroad cars full of granite, limestone, and other materials to make the capitol building. The building materials cost $3.7 million. The builder of the capitol wasn't paid in money. He was given three million acres of land in the Texas Panhandle area. That was enough land to cover ten Texas counties.

The University of Texas at Austin is close to the capitol. About 50,000 students attend the university. The Lyndon Baines Johnson Presidential Library is located on the university's campus. Here, you can learn about the 36th president and read a few of the forty-two million important papers stored here!

Lots of musicians live and play in Austin. It is sometimes called the "live music capital of the world." The PBS TV show "Austin City Limits" is broadcast from there. 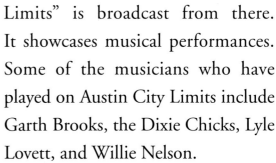 It showcases musical performances. Some of the musicians who have played on Austin City Limits include Garth Brooks, the Dixie Chicks, Lyle Lovett, and Willie Nelson.

Go south and you'll get one of the nicest views of the city at Louis Neff Point. This is where Barton Creek flows into the Colorado River. You can watch the river flow right through the city. Barton Creek is dammed up in Zilker Park to form

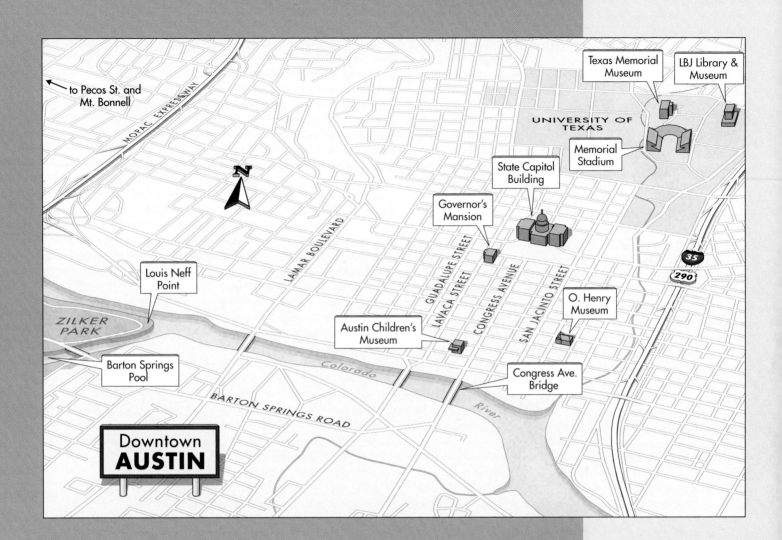

to Pecos St. and
Mt. Bonnell

MOPAC EXPRESSWAY

UNIVERSITY OF
TEXAS

Texas Memorial
Museum

LBJ Library &
Museum

Memorial
Stadium

State Capitol
Building

Governor's
Mansion

N

LAMAR BOULEVARD

Louis Neff
Point

ZILKER
PARK

GUADALUPE STREET

LAVACA STREET

CONGRESS AVENUE

SAN JACINTO STREET

O. Henry
Museum

35

290

Austin Children's
Museum

Colorado

Barton Springs
Pool

Congress Ave.
Bridge

BARTON SPRINGS ROAD

River

Downtown
AUSTIN

Barton Springs. This popular 900-foot long pool stays a cool 68°F (20°C) year round.

If you like bats, Austin is your city. As the sun goes down, you can see more than a million Mexican free-tail bats fly out from under the Congress Avenue Bridge. These bats eat about 14,000 pounds of insects each day. Austin folks even named their hockey team the Austin Ice Bats!

At night from March to November, Mexican free-tail bats fly out from under the Congress Avenue bridge.

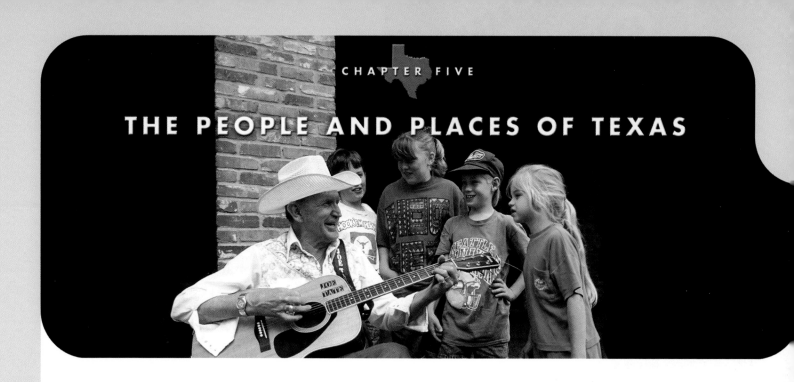

CHAPTER FIVE

THE PEOPLE AND PLACES OF TEXAS

Texas's huge spaces and rugged land has shaped its people. Even today, Texans are known for being independent yet friendly. Over hundreds of years, Texas has drawn people from all over the world. That is still true today. Almost twenty-one million people live in the Lone Star State. Almost eight out of ten Texans are Caucasian. About twelve out of a hundred Texans are African-American, about two out of a hundred are Asian, and less than one out of a hundred is Native American. Another ten out of a hundred are of other racial backgrounds.

Many of Texas's Native Americans live in cities. However, Texas still has three reservations. Two of them welcome visitors. You can go to see Alabama-Coushatta Reservation in the Big Thicket National Preserve and the Tigua Reservation near El Paso in west Texas. The Texas Band of Traditional Kickapoo also have a reservation along the Rio Grande River at Eagle Pass.

A musician entertains visitors at Market Square in downtown San Antonio.

Nearly three out of ten Texans say that they are Hispanic. Many of these people can trace their families back to when Texas was part of Mexico. In some Texas border towns, Spanish is the main language. Mexican music and festivals are common throughout the state. Even more common is tasty Mexican food.

Many people in Texas can trace their ancestry back to Mexican settlers. This teen-ager is trying on a sombrero.

Although not large in number, African-Americans play a big part in the life of Texas. Until the Civil War, most of Texas's African-Americans were enslaved people. In recent years, Texas African-Americans, such as former Congresswoman Barbara Jordan, actress and producer Debbie Allen, boxing champion George Foreman, actor and producer Jamie Foxx, and actress Phylicia Rashad have made names for themselves in politics, sports, and the arts.

In Texas a celebration known as Juneteenth honors the emancipation of enslaved people in Texas.

N

0   50   100 mi.
0   50   100 km

OKLAHOMA

ARKANSAS

NEW MEXICO

Amarillo

Lubbock

El Paso

Fort Worth   Dallas

Abilene

San Angelo

Waco

LOUISIANA

Austin

Houston

San Antonio

Galveston

MEXICO

Laredo

Corpus Christi

Gulf
of
Mexico

	Cattle		Fruit		Rice
	Chemicals		Iron ore		Sheep
	Cotton		Manufacturing		Shrimp
	Dairy		Natural gas		Uranium
	Fish		Oil		Vegetables

Since pioneer days, women have played an important part in Texas's history. In this century, Miriam "Ma" Ferguson became the first woman governor in the United States in 1925-1927. She was later elected to a second term, from 1933-1935. Ferguson fought the Ku Klux Klan, a secret organization that had threatened, attacked, and killed many African-Americans. She also fought to help poor people during the Great Depression. Later, Ann Richards followed in her footsteps by serving as governor from 1991-1995. The National Cowgirl Museum and Hall of Fame in Fort Worth, Texas, celebrates a different kind of western women's achievement. It shows the trophies and riding costumes of more than one hundred female rodeo stars. Yee-haw!

Many groups of immigrants came to settle in Texas. Some of the newest residents of Texas are from Asia. Among them are Vietnamese people who make their living fishing along the Gulf of Mexico, and Japanese people who are rice farmers near Houston. Other members of Texas's Asian population work in all kinds of areas, from computers to fashion and beyond.

Texans are mostly urban people—they live in cities or towns. Only about one-fifth of all Texans live in rural areas. The population is more tightly packed toward the eastern part of the state. Houston is the largest city in Texas, followed by San Antonio, Dallas, El Paso, and Austin. In fact, Texas has three of the largest cities in the United States.

The official dish of Texas is chili con carne. This "Tex-Mex" dish became famous in San Antonio. Women called "Chili Queens" once sold plates of chili with a tortilla for a dime. Now, a former ghost town, Terlingua is the home of the famous International Chili Championship. Here's a chili recipe to try yourself. Remember, get a grown-up to help you!

CHILI CON CARNE

1 tablespoon olive oil

2 cups chopped onions

1 chopped green bell pepper

1 pound lean ground beef

Two 15 oz. cans kidney or pinto beans

One 14-oz. can of pasta-ready tomatoes

6 oz. can tomato paste

2 cups water

3 tablespoons chili powder

2 tablespoon cider vinegar

2 teaspoons sliced garlic

2 teaspoons oregano

2 teaspoon cumin

1/2 teaspoon freshly ground black pepper

1 bay leaf

1. Heat oil in a skillet over medium-high heat.
2. Add onion and pepper. Cook until onion is soft. Add meat and sauté until brown. Pour off all fat.
3. Add beans and remaining ingredients, including water, and heat until boiling.
4. Reduce heat to low and cook for one hour, stirring occasionally. Remove bay leaf before serving.

Working on an oil rig is long and hard work.

(opposite bottom)
A worker fills an airplane's fuel tank.

WORKING IN TEXAS

Texas has led the United States in creating jobs in recent years. Texas has so many workers that about seven out of every hundred jobs exist in Texas. Texans do all kinds of work, from computer software design to ranching.

Almost from its beginning, Texas has been known for its ranches and farms. At one time, that's where most Texans worked. Texas still has about 200,000 farms, more than any other state. More than 15 million cattle graze on Texas ranchland. Many people also raise crops, such as wheat, grapefruit, and cotton.

Texas leads the nation in the production of oil and natural gas. There is oil under about two-thirds of Texas land. Many people have found jobs in the oil and natural gas fields.

Texas factories change the oil into fuel and chemicals. In fact, chemicals are Texas's leading factory products. Thousands of items are made from petroleum and natural gas. Some of these products are explosives, cosmetics, paint, and fertilizers.

Those are not the only things that Texans make. Food processing is another big business. Grain, beef, fruits, vegetables, chickens, and milk are processed in Texas. Then they are shipped to markets around the world. About twelve out of every hundred Texans work in manufacturing.

Almost three out of ten jobs in Texas are in the service industries. That means these jobs are in sales, banking, real estate, and insurance. Other service workers are bank tellers, bus drivers, and state park employees.

Texas is a leader in computer manufacturing. Many people are moving to Texas to find high-tech jobs. A space technology industry has sprung up around Houston's Lyndon B. Johnson Space Center. Factory workers make space equipment, rockets, and other items needed in space. One Houston company, called Celestis, has started a business of space burial. People can send small capsules of their loved one's ashes to outer space for the price of $5,600 each. One of the first person's ashes to be sent up were those of Texas-born Gene Roddenberry. He created the TV show "Star Trek."

Technology even helps the fishing industry. Pollution and overfishing have decreased the fish population in the Gulf

Oil refineries process crude oil into useful products, such as fuel oil, gasoline, or kerosene.

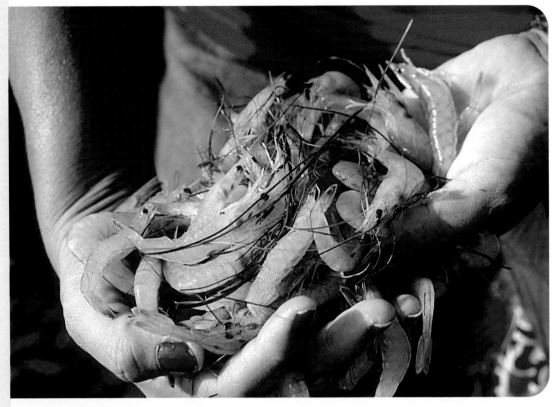

A worker holds shrimp harvested on an aquaculture farm.

This scientist holds shrimp raised on farms in the water. Most shrimp farms are located along the Gulf Coast; however, there are some successful aquafarms in West Texas.

Coast. Now, experts are turning to aquaculture to help grow a larger population of these creatures. Fish are raised and harvested on farms in the water. Shrimp and catfish are only two kinds of fish produced this way.

Movie making is another large Texas business. More than 900 movies and TV shows have been made in Texas. Movies include "Apollo 13" and "Toy Soldiers." TV shows that have been filmed in Texas are "Wishbone," "Walker, Texas Ranger," and "Barney."

Many people also find jobs in the tourist industry. Tourists spend about $20.6 billion a year visiting Texas's state parks, recreation areas, and other interesting places. Many people are employed helping these visitors. Some helpers are among the seventeen percent of Texans who work for the government.

Tourists can find all kinds of things to do in Texas from camping in the mountains at a national park to touring an old Spanish mission. These people are enjoying a roller coaster ride in San Antonio.

This view shows the moon over the Dallas skyline.

Northeast Texas

Starting in the high plains of North Texas you can visit two large cities—Dallas and Fort Worth. These two cities, called the "Metroplex," share an airport and sports teams like the Texas Rangers and the Dallas Cowboys. However, each city has a completely different feeling. Dallas is known for its gleaming skyscrapers, fashion, and wealth. It is home to

Crowds gather at an outdoor Thanksgiving celebration in Dallas.

the ultra-glamorous Neiman Marcus Department Store. Fort Worth is "where the West begins," according to many. That's because it has a different, more rough-and-ready feeling than genteel Dallas. Cattle drives once stopped in Fort Worth. It had a large meat packing industry. Later, many Fort Worth citizens became rich through the oil industry. Now it has the huge Amon Carter Museum of Western Art—and it still has rodeos to this day.

Southeastern Texas and Gulf Coast

Eastern Texas is bordered by Louisiana. This area has many pine forests and large cotton farms. Going south, this part of Texas borders the Gulf of Mexico. The state has 367 miles (590.6 km) of coastline. One of the most beautiful places along the coast is Padre Island National Seashore. It is a sandy island right off the Texas coast. Animals such as sea turtles, coyotes, and snakes make their homes on its white sand beaches and grasslands.

FIND OUT MORE

In the late 1800s, cowboys herded cattle to Fort Worth. They stopped on their way to the railroad depots. The stockyards at Fort Worth were the largest in the world. How might Fort Worth's location have helped it to develop and to thrive?

Padre Island is a barrier along the Texas coast between Port Isabel and Corpus Christi.

NEW MEXICO

OKLAHOMA

ARKANSAS

LOUISIANA

MEXICO

Gulf
of
Mexico

RITA BLANCA
NAT'L GRASSLAND

Amarillo
Zoo

40 40
Amarillo

Buffalo Lake
Nat'l Wildlife
Refuge

27

Lubbock

Copper Breaks
State Park

35

30

Fort Worth
Dallas

Cow Town
Rodeo

Six Flags
Over Texas

20

Big Spring
State Park

20
Abilene

Dinosaur Valley
State Park

SABINE
NAT'L
FOREST

El Paso

GUADALUPE MTNS.
NATIONAL PARK

San Angelo

Waco

DAVY
CROCKETT
NAT'L
FOREST

ANGELINA
NAT'L
FOREST

10

10

35

45

SAM HOUSTON
NAT'L FOREST

BIG
THICKET NAT'L
PRESERVE

Seminole Canyon
State Historical Park

BIG BEND
NATIONAL
PARK

Amistad National
Recreation
Area

Barton Creek
Trail

Austin

Houston

San Jacinto Battleground
State Historical Park

10

San Antonio

Sea World
of Texas

San Antonio Zoo

Alamo

10

Lyndon B. Johnson
Space Center
NASA

Galveston

Galveston Island
Beach

ARANSAS NAT'L
WILDLIFE
REFUGE

35

37

Laredo

Corpus Christi

Mustang Island State Park

PADRE ISLAND
NATIONAL
SEASHORE

Bentsen-Rio
Grande Valley
State Park

Sabal Palm Grove
Wildlife Sanctuary

N

0   50   100 mi.

0   50   100 km

Legend

National forest, seashore, wildlife
refuge, or marine sanctuary

Highway

⊛ Capital city

• City

🌲 State park (not all shown)

■ Tourist site

Houston is located in eastern Texas. It's the fourth largest city in the United States. It is an important center for the oil industry and space program. This exciting city has lots of attractions, such as the Museum of Texas History and Space Center Houston. Astronauts train at the Lyndon B. Johnson Space Center. At the space museum you can learn about how astronauts train and try on space suits.

Houston can be hot and steamy, but it has miles of air-conditioned tunnels that people can use to walk from store to store downtown. It also has restaurants with food from all over the world.

Many of Houston's sports teams play in the Astrodome. Opening in 1965, it was the first ball park in the United States to have air-conditioning.

(bottom left)
Houston's National League team, the Astros, play on Enron Field at the Ballpark at Union Station.

(bottom right)
The Astrodome, in Houston, contains about 5,000 plastic skylights. Between 55,000 to 76,000 people can be seated in this stadium.

The Houston Ship Channel helped to turn Houston into a major port. Millions of barrels of oil are shipped from Houston to locations around the world.

Houston is more than fifty miles from the Gulf of Mexico. However, it is an important ocean port because it has a 52-mile long ship channel that transports thousands of ships every year. The channel is like a small river that leads from Houston to the Gulf. Many of these ships carry oil from nearby refineries.

Austin, the capital city, is located in the Hill Country of central Texas. So are the towns of New Braunfels and Fredericksburg. These towns were founded by German immigrants. Many people come to Fredericksburg for a big fair called Oktoberfest, where German food and heritage is celebrated. You can listen to polka music, sample bites of sausage, and see arts and crafts there. If you get too hot, you can cool off at the Schlitterbahn in New Braunfels. It is a waterpark whose name means "slippery road" in German! You can go on lots of fun rides and slippery slides like the Boogie Bahn Surfing Wave and the Dragon Blaster Uphill Water coaster.

San Antonio was founded as a mission in 1718. Many visitors come here to tour the Alamo, the state's top attraction. First, you can see the chapel where the defenders of the Alamo died. Then you can go to the

WHO'S WHO IN TEXAS?

Buddy Holly (1936-1959). Born in Lubbock, Buddy Holly was one of rock and roll's pioneers. His songs, such as "Peggy Sue," influenced later musicians. The twenty-three year old singer died in a plane crash.

This view shows the San Antonio skyline.

67

Visitors can tour the Alamo, a symbol of Texas pride and independence. Inside, an exhibit displays some personal items belonging to the men who died there.

Long Barracks Museum. There, you can hear a narration about the fall of the Alamo, and see mementos of the event. The Alamo is surrounded by a lovely plaza.

You can also come to the market square area called El Mercado, which features Mexican restaurants and stores with Mexican crafts. You might glide through the city on a boat on San Antonio's Paseo del Río (River Walk). The 21-block area is open to pedestrians. It is built along the San Antonio River and is lined with pretty shops and restaurants. You can cross over the walkways on small bridges. People ride water taxis or paddleboats up and down the river.

The city is home to the San Antonio Spurs basketball team and the San Antonio Missions basketball team. The Spurs play in a basketball arena called the Alamo-dome, which also includes two permanent ice skating rinks.

Southwest

As you travel south and west, you notice that the landscape changes once again. The surroundings look more like a desert. Few people live in this region. However, the area isn't empty. It is home to more than seventy types of animals and four hundred kinds of birds. They include roadrunners, kit foxes, pumas, mule deer, and peregrine falcons.

El Paso is the westernmost city in Texas. It's a great place to buy cowboy boots or to look at murals. Murals, wall paintings, are all over the city. Many of them have Mexican themes. El Paso is the largest border city on the Rio Grande. Visitors can cross a bridge to Ciudad Juárez, Mexico, the city across the border, for a day trip.

Northwest and Panhandle

Heading northwest, you arrive in the Texas Panhandle. Among the major industries here are cattle ranching and oil drilling. The main cities are Lubbock and Amarillo.

One of the Panhandle's most beautiful attractions is Palo Duro Canyon south of Amarillo. It has been called the Grand Canyon of Texas. The bottom of the canyon is 800 feet (244 m) below its rim. In the summer, the play *Texas* is performed right in the canyon.

The huge rock formation is known as Lighthouse Rock in Palo Duro Canyon. *Texas*, a musical play, is presented on a 600-foot cliff where about eighty singers and dancers perform.

TEXAS ALMANAC

Statehood date and number: December 29, 1845; the 28th state

State seal (date adopted): first version, 1836, most currently adapted version 1991

State flag (date adopted): 1839

Total Area: 267,277 miles (692,247 km)

Greatest distance north to south: 737 miles (1,186 km)

Greatest distance east to west: 774 miles (1,245 km)

Borders: Mexico, New Mexico, Oklahoma, Arkansas, Louisiana, and the Gulf of Mexico.

Highest/lowest elevation: Guadalupe Peak, 8,749 feet (2,668 m); Gulf of Mexico, Sea Level

Hottest/coldest temperature: 120°F (49°C) (August 12, 1936)/-23°F (February 8, 1938) (-30.5°C)

Population and rank: 20,851,820 (2000 Census), second most populous state

Origin of state name: *Tejas,* which means friends in the Caddo language

Capital and earlier capitals: Austin. Earlier capitals include: Washington-on-Brazos, Houston, San Felipe de Austin, Saltillo, Monclova, Columbia, Harrisburg

Counties: 254 counties

State government: 31 Senators, 150 Representatives

Major Rivers, Lakes: Rio Grande and Colorado Rivers, Lake Sam Rayburn (114,500 acres) and Toledo Bend Reservoir (181,000 acres)

Farm products: cattle, sheep, grain sorghums, cotton, wheat, rice, dairy products, grapefruit

Manufactured products: chemical products, petroleum products, food products, and transportation equipment

Mining products: petroleum, natural gas

Fishing products: shrimp, catfish

Population of major cities: (2000 Census): Houston, 1,953,631; Dallas, 1,188,580; San Antonio, 1,144,646; Austin, 656,562; El Paso, 563,662; Fort Worth, 534,694

Nickname: The Lone Star State

Motto: Friendship

Flower: Bluebonnet

Bird: Mockingbird

Tree: Pecan

Song: "Texas, Our Texas" (1929), composed by William J. Marsh (lyrics by Marsh and Gladys Yoakum Wright)

Gem: Blue Topaz

Dish: Chili

Dinosaur: Brachiosaur, Sauropod, Pleurocoelus

Large Mammal: Longhorn

Musical Instrument: Guitar

Native Pepper: Chiltepin

Pepper: Jalapeño

Plant: Prickly Pear Cactus

Plays: *The Lone Star, Texas, Beyond the Sundown, Fandangle*

Reptile: Horned Lizard

Seashell: Lightning Whelk

Ship: U.S.S. Texas

Small Mammal: Armadillo

Sport: Rodeo

Stone: Petrified Palmwood

Vegetable: Sweet Texas Onion

Coastline: 367 miles; (590.6 km) Shoreline: 3,359 miles (5405.8 km)

Fiber and Fabric: Cotton

Fish: Guadalupe Bass

Flying Mammal: Mexican Free-Tail Bat

Folk Dance: Square Dance

Fruit: Red Grapefruit

Gemstone Cut: Lone Star Cut

Grass: Sideoats Grama

Insect: Monarch Butterfly

TIME**LINE**

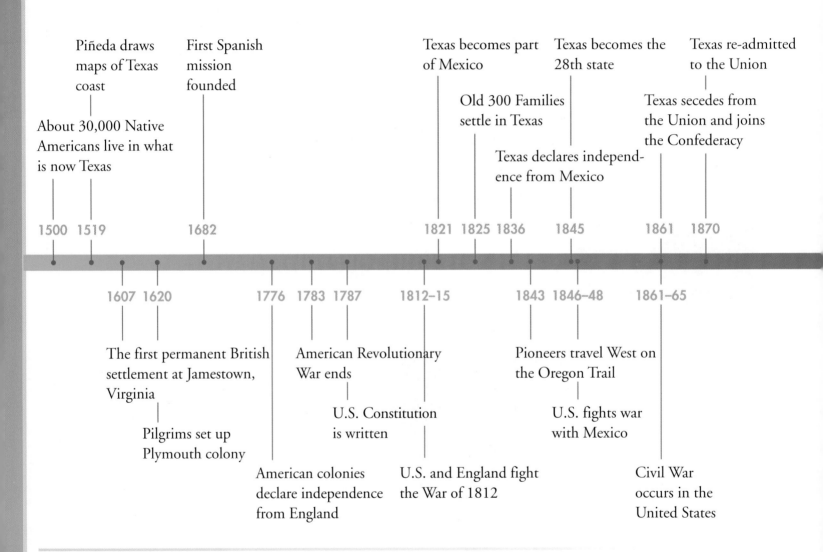

Piñeda draws maps of Texas coast

First Spanish mission founded

Texas becomes part of Mexico

Texas becomes the 28th state

Texas re-admitted to the Union

Old 300 Families settle in Texas

Texas secedes from the Union and joins the Confederacy

About 30,000 Native Americans live in what is now Texas

Texas declares independence from Mexico

1500　**1519**　　　　　**1682**　　　　　　　**1821**　**1825**　**1836**　　**1845**　　　　**1861**　**1870**

1607 1620　　　　**1776 1783 1787**　　**1812–15**　　　**1843 1846–48**　　**1861–65**

The first permanent British settlement at Jamestown, Virginia

American Revolutionary War ends

Pioneers travel West on the Oregon Trail

Pilgrims set up Plymouth colony

U.S. Constitution is written

U.S. fights war with Mexico

American colonies declare independence from England

U.S. and England fight the War of 1812

Civil War occurs in the United States

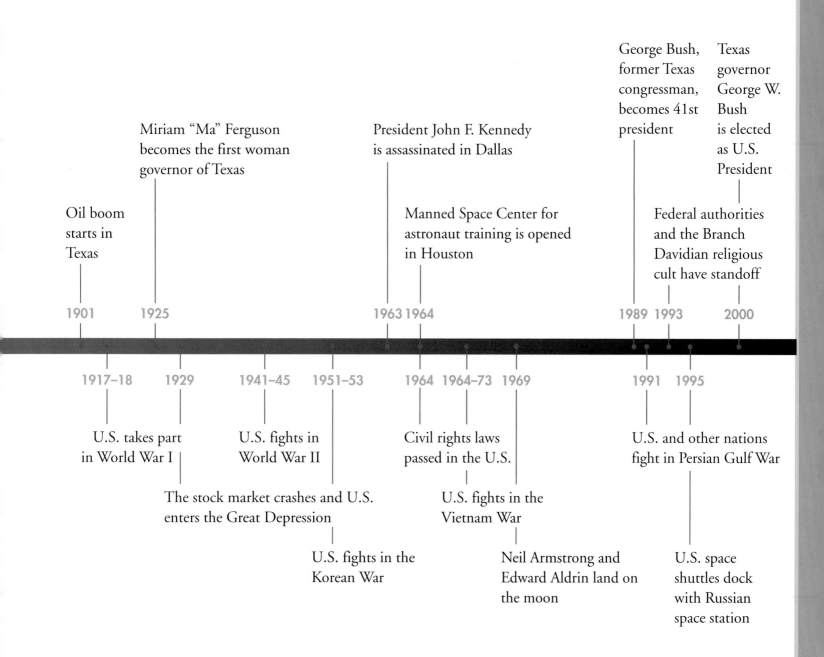

Oil boom
starts in
Texas

Miriam "Ma" Ferguson
becomes the first woman
governor of Texas

President John F. Kennedy
is assassinated in Dallas

Manned Space Center for
astronaut training is opened
in Houston

George Bush,
former Texas
congressman,
becomes 41st
president

Texas
governor
George W.
Bush
is elected
as U.S.
President

Federal authorities
and the Branch
Davidian religious
cult have standoff

1901   1925   1963 1964   1989 1993   2000

1917–18   1929   1941–45   1951–53   1964   1964–73   1969   1991   1995

U.S. takes part
in World War I

U.S. fights in
World War II

Civil rights laws
passed in the U.S.

U.S. and other nations
fight in Persian Gulf War

The stock market crashes and U.S.
enters the Great Depression

U.S. fights in the
Vietnam War

U.S. fights in the
Korean War

Neil Armstrong and
Edward Aldrin land on
the moon

U.S. space
shuttles dock
with Russian
space station

GALLERY OF FAMOUS TEXANS

Alvin Ailey
(1931–1989)
Award-winning dancer and choreographer. Born in Rogers.

Oveta Culp Hobby
(1905–1995)
First U.S. Secretary of Health, Education and Welfare (1953–55). Born in Killeen.

Kay Bailey Hutchison
(1944–   )
First woman to represent Texas in the U.S. Senate. Grew up in LaMarque.

Quanah Parker
(1845?–1911)
Comanche warrior and chief. Worked to improve living conditions for his people.

Jennifer Love Hewitt
(1979–   )
Singer and TV and movie actress. Born in Waco.

José Antonio Navarro
(1795–1871)
A politician who helped to create the first state constitution. Born in San Antonio.

Sandra Day O'Connor
(1930–   )
First woman to serve on the U.S. Supreme Court. Born in El Paso.

Dan Rather
(1931–   )
TV newscaster who's covered many national and international events. Born in Wharton.

Nolan Ryan
(1947–   )
All-time great baseball pitcher who struck out 5,714 batters and pitched seven no-hitters. Born in Refugio.

Lorenzo de Zavala
(1788–1836)
Texas Republic's first vice president, fighter for democracy.

GLOSSARY

adobe: sun-dried mud bricks

assassinate: to kill a prominent person

bison: buffalo

boundary: a line that separates two places

Buffalo Soldiers: African-American soldiers who fought in the Indian wars after 1865

canyon: a narrow, deep valley, with steep, tall sides

coast: land that borders on the sea or ocean

Confederate: belonging to the 11 states that withdrew from the United States in 1861

drought: a long dry period when rain doesn't fall

escarpment: a line of steep slopes or cliffs

extinct: no longer in existence

fertile: rich in material that supports life

glacier: large body of ice that moves slowly down a mountain

granite: a very hard, pretty kind of rock

irrigate: to provide water for crops through a system of ditches

javelina: a kind of wild pig

mammoths: extinct elephants that were covered with hair

maverick: an independent individual who does not follow the crowd

mohair: the smooth, soft hair of Angora goats

nomadic: moving from place to place

panhandle: a narrow piece of land that extends out of the larger territory it belongs to

plain: broad stretch of land or almost level land

plateau: a high, level, piece of land

prairie: a large area of grassland

recourse: source of help

reservoir: an artificial lake where water is kept for human use

secede: withdraw from

segregation: the forced separation of people by race, gender, or ethnic background

sorghum: a grain used for making a sweet syrup

sovereign nation: an independent nation

territory: a geographical area controlled by a government

Texian: Early residents of Texas who sought independence

tributary: stream or river that flows into a larger river

valley: long, low area of land, usually between mountains of high hills

vaquero: cowboy in Spanish

FOR MORE INFORMATION

Web sites

The Handbook of Texas Online
http://www.tsha.utexas.edu/handbook/online
This website is an encyclopedia of Texas history, geography, and culture.

Texas Almanac
http://www.texasalmanac.com
This site is a great source of up-to-date information.

Texas for Visitors
http://gotexas.about.com/travel/gotexas/mbody.htm
This informative site about Texas has lots of links.

Texas Treasures
http://www.tsl.state.tx.us/treasures/index.html
The site is sponsored by the Texas State Library and Archives Commission.

Texas Senate
http://www.senate.state.tx.us/kids/Tour.htm
Take a virtual tour of the state capitol building on this web site.

Books

Heinrichs, Ann, *Texas,* Children's Press, 1999.

Kent, Deborah, *Dallas,* Children's Press, 2000.

Rita Kerr, *The Alamo Cat*, Eakin Publications, 1987.

Lourie, Peter, *Rio Grande*, Boyds Mills Press, 1999.

Sanford, William R., *The Chisholm Trail in American History,* Enslow Publishers, 2000.

Santella, Andrew, *The Battle of the Alamo,* Children's Press, 1997.

Address

Texas Department of Transportation/Travel Division
P.O. Box 4249
Austin, TX 78714-9249
1-800-452-9292
You can ask for free tourist guides and maps.

INDEX

Page numbers in *italics* indicate illustrations

air pollution, 40
airplane refueling, *59*
Alabama-Coushatta Reservation, 53
Alamo, 27–28, *28*, 67–68, *68*
Alamodome, 68
Alvin Ailey Dance Troupe, *42*
Angelina National Forest, 15
Angora (goats), 12
aquaculture, 60
Astrodome, *65*, 66
astronauts, 39
Austin, 47, 50–52, *51*
Austin, Stephen F., 24, *24*, 26, 29

Balcones Escarpment, 10
barbed wire, 35
bats, 52, *52*
Battle of San Jacinto, 28
Big Bend National Park, *7, 9, 9, 14*, 40
Big Thicket National Preserve, 53
Bill of Rights, 43
Borden, Gail, 25, *25*
boundaries, 32
Brazos River, 15
Buffalo Soldiers, 36
Bush, George (father), 40
Bush, George W. (son), 40, *45*

Caddo Lake, 15
Caddoans, 18–19
Cap Rock Escarpment, 12
capital of Texas, 47, 50–52, *51*
capitol building, 47, 50
cattle drives, 34–36, *35*
Celestis. *See* space burial
Central Plains, 10, 12
central Texas, 67–69
chemical factories, 58
chili con carne (food), 57
Chisos Mountains, *14*

Civil Rights, 38–39
Civil War, *33*, 33–34
climate, 13, 15–17
Coastal Plains, 10
Colorado River, 15
Comal River, 15
Compromise of 1850, 32
computer manufacturing, 59
Confederate States of America, 33
Congress Avenue Bridge, *52*
Constitution, 43
Coronado, Francisco Vasquez de, *20*, 20–21
Corsicana, 36–37
court system, 46–47
covered wagons, *25*
cowboys, 34–36
Crockett, Davy, 27, *27*
Cullinan, J. S., 37
cultural diversity, 32

Dallas, *62*, 62–63
Declaration of Independence, 27–28
Dell Computers, 42
droughts, 16, 17, 38
Dust Bowl, 38
dust storms, 16

economy, 41
Eisenhower, Dwight D., 38, *38*
El Mercado, 68
El Paso, 69
Enchanted Rock, 68
escarpments, 10, 12
Estevanico (African explorer), 20
executive branch, 44–45
explorers, 20–21

factories, 38
famous people, 41–42, 50, 54, *65*, 67
Farmer, James, 39
farming, 12, 18–19, 33, 56, 58
Ferguson, Miriam "Ma," 56

fishing industry, 56, 59–60
flags, 4
food processing, 58
forests, 10
    Angelina National Forest, 15
Fort St. Louis, 21
Fort Worth, 63
free-tail bats, 52

geography, 7–13
Goddess of Liberty, 50
government, 43–47, 48
governors, 49
Grand Canyon of Texas, 69
Granger, Gordon, 34
Great Depression, 38
Great Plains, 12
gross state product, 41
Gulf Coast, 63, 65–66
Gulf of Mexico, 63, 66

Hamm, Mia, 41–42
Hasinai Confederacy, 19
Henry, O., 50
herding, 23. See also ranching
Hill Country, 67
Holly, Buddy, 67
Houston, 65–66
Houston, Sam, 28, 28–29, 29, 30, 31,
    33
Houston Astros, 66
Houston Ship Channel, 66
hurricanes, 16

immigrants. See people
independence
    from Mexico, 27–28
    of Texas, 43
Indian reservations, 36, 53
industries, 41
inventions
    barbed wire, 35
    condensed milk, 25
irrigation, 12

jobs, 58–61
Johnson, Lyndon Baines, 39, 39

Joplin, Scott, 56
judicial branch, 46–47
Juneteenth, 34, 54

Kennedy, John F., 39
King Ranch, 35–36
Ku Klux Klan, 56

La Salle, Rene-Robert Cavelier, Sieur de,
    21
La Salle shipwreck, 21
lakes and reservoirs, 15
Lamar, Mirabeau, 30
landforms, 7–13
law and order, 29
legislative branch, 44
Lighthouse Rock, 69
livestock, 34–36
longhorn cattle, 23, 23, 34–36, 35
lumber industry, 10
Lyndon B. Johnson Space Center. See
    Space Center
Lyndon Baines Johnson Presidential
    Library,
    50

Manned Space Center. See Space Center
manufacturing, 58–59
maps
    Austin, 51
    highway, 64
    natural resource, 6
    political, 55
    topographical, 11
Maverick, Sam, 36
Metroplex, 62
Mexican-American war, 32
Mexican dancing, 50
Mexican free-tail bats, 52
Mexico
    independence from Spain, 24
    tensions with settlers, 26
Mission de la Ysleta, 23
missionaries, 22
mountain ranges, 13
movie making, 60
Murphy, Audie, 38

museums
    Amon Carter Museum of Western Art, 63
    Hall of Fame, 56
    Long Barracks Museum, 68
    Museum of Texas History, 65
    National Cowgirl Museum, 56
    Permian Basin Petroleum Museum, 12
    Space Center Houston, 66
music, 50
musician at Market Square, *53*

Native Americans, 19, 36
natural gas, 58
natural resources, 12, 37, 58
Navarro, Jose Antonio, 43
Northeast Texas, 62–63
Northwest Texas, 69

oil
    discovery, 36–37
    oil well, *13*
    refineries, 58, *59*
    rig workers, *58*
Oktoberfest, 67
Old Three Hundred, 24
Padre Island National Seashore, 63, *63*
Palo Duro Canyon, 69, *69*
Panhandle, 8, 69
paper mills, 10
pelicans, *17*
people, 53–54, 56
    arrival of immigrants, 25, 32
    Asian immigrants, 56
    early inhabitants, 18–19
    European explorers, 20–21
    famous, 41–42, 50, 54, *65*, 67
    Native Americans, 36, 53
    Old Three Hundred, 24
    population increase, 31–32
    settlers and Native American hostility, 30–31
    settlers in the 1800s, 24–26, 30
    Texians, 26–28
Permian Basin, 12, *13*
physical regions, 7–13
pictographs, 18

Pineda, Alonso Alvarez de, 20
Polk, James, 31
pollution, 40–41
population increase, 31–32
Porter, William Henry, 50
Puebloans, 19

ranching, 12, 34–36, 58
Red River, 15
Republic of Texas, 4, 29–31
Richards, Anne, 56
Rio Grande, *8*, 14, 41
rivers, 14–15
Riverwalk, 68
Roddenberry, Gene, 59
roller coaster riders, *61*

Sam Rayburn Reservoir, 15
San Angelo, 12
San Antonio, 67–68
    skyline, *67*
San Felipe de Austin, 24
sand castle, *9*
Santa Anna, Antonio Lopez de, 26, 27, 28
Schlitterbahn waterpark, 67
segregation, 38–39
service industries, 59
settlers
    hostility with Native Americans, 30–31
    in the 1800s, 30
    tensions with Mexico, 26
    Texians, 26–28
settlers in the 1800s, 24–26
shrimp, *60*
slavery, 33, 34
sombrero, *54*
Soto, Hernando de, 21
Southeastern Texas, 63, 65–66
Southwest Texas, 68–69
space burial, 59
Space Center, 39, 59
space technology, 59
Spanish missions, 22
Spindletop oil field, 37, *37*
sports, 66, 68

Star Trek, 59
State of Texas, 31

television, 60
Texaco, Inc., 37
Texas Band of Traditional Kickapoo, 53
Texas Fuel Company, 37
Texas Rangers, 29, *30*
Texas revolution, 27
Texas State Fair, *40*
Texians, 26–28
Thanksgiving celebration, *62*
Tigua Reservation, 53
Toledo Bend Reservoir, 15
Tornado Alley, 16
tornadoes, 16
touring Texas, 62–69
tourism, 61
trade, 41
Trans-Pecos Region, 13
Travis, William B., 27

U. S. Congress for Racial Equality, 39
University of Texas, 50

Vaca, Alvar Nunez Cabeza de, 20, *21*

water pollution, 40–41
weather. *See* climate
women. *See also* famous people
  in Texas history, 56
  during World War II, 38
Wool and Mohair Capital, 12
World War I, 37
World War II, 38

Zaharias, Mildred "Babe" Didrikson, *65*

MEET THE AUTHOR

Alexandra Hanson-Harding lives in New Jersey with her husband, Brian, and her sons, Moses and Jacob. Alexandra works full-time as a writer. She has written hundreds of articles for kids and five books for kids and teachers. To write this book, she read everything she could get her hands on about Texas, mostly from books, magazines, the Internet, and other sources.

Photographs: AllSport USA/Brian Bahr: 66 bottom; Archive Photos: 74 bottom left (CNP), 42, 59 bottom; Buddy Mays/Travel Stock: 13, 53, 61, 67; Byron Augustin: 4, 22; Corbis-Bettmann: 59 top (Marilyn Bridges), 17 (Richard Cummins), 65 bottom (Henry Diltz), 60 bottom (Lowell Georgia), 68 (Dave G. Houser), 50, 54 top (Kelly-Mooney Photography), 9 bottom (Left Lane Productions), 7 top, 60 top (Buddy Mays), 71 bottom left (Joe McDonald), 71 bottom right, 14, 63, 69 (David Muench), 74 right (Pacha), 8 (Chris Rainier), cover, 3 right (H. David Seawell), 70 bottom, 18 (Joseph Sohm:ChromoSohm), 58 (Jim Sugar Photography), 12, 71 top left (Roger Tidman), 24 bottom, 25 bottom, 27, 28 bottom, 29, 37, 38, 39, 65 top, 74 top left; Courtesy of the Texas Secretary of State: 70 top; D. Donne Bryant Stock Photography: 43, 44; Dallas Convention & Visitors Bureau: 62 bottom, 71 top right; North Wind Picture Archives: 20, 25 top, 34; Panhandle-Plains Historical Museum: 30; Photo Researchers, NY: 71 center left (Nigel Cattlin/Holt Studios), 23 (Francois Gohier), 52 (Karen Marks), 71 left (David M. Schleser/Natures Images, Inc.); Stock Montage, Inc.: 21, 24 top, 28 top, 33, 35; Stone: 45, 54 bottom (Robert E. Daemmrich), 62 top (John Elk), 3 left, 7 bottom, 9 top (David Muench), 40 (Peter Poulides), 66 top (Keith Wood).